INSECTS & SPIDERS

GIANT SPIDERS & INSECTS

Chris McNab

GARETH**STEVENS**
GS
P U B L I S H I N G
A Member of the WRC Media Family of Companies

D1709899

Please visit our Web site at: **www.garethstevens.com**
For a free color catalog describing Gareth Stevens Publishing's
list of high-quality books and multimedia programs,
call 1-800-542-2595 (USA) or 1-800-387-3178 (Canada).
Gareth Stevens Publishing's fax: (414) 332-3567.

Library of Congress Cataloging-in-Publication Data

McNab, Chris.
    Giant spiders & insects / Chris McNab.
        p. cm. — (Nature's monsters. Insects & spiders)
    Includes bibliographical references and index.
    ISBN-10: 0-8368-6850-1 — ISBN-13: 978-0-8368-6850-0 (lib. bdg.)
    1. Spiders—Size—Juvenile literature. 2. Insects—Size—Juvenile literature. I. Title:
Giant spiders and insects. II. Title. III. Series.
    QL458.4M44   2006
    595.4'4—dc22   2006042383

This North American edition first published in 2007 by
Gareth Stevens Publishing
A Member of the WRC Media Family of Companies
330 West Olive Street, Suite 100
Milwaukee, WI 53212 USA

Original edition and illustrations copyright © 2006 by International Masters Publishers AB.
Produced by Amber Books Ltd., Bradley's Close, 74–77 White Lion Street, London N1 9PF, U.K.

Project editor: Michael Spilling
Design: Joe Conneally

Gareth Stevens editorial direction: Valerie J. Weber
Gareth Stevens editor: Leifa Butrick
Gareth Stevens art direction: Tammy West
Gareth Stevens production: Jessica Morris

Printed in the United States of America

1 2 3 4 5 6 7 8 9 10 09 08 07 06

Contents

Continents of the World

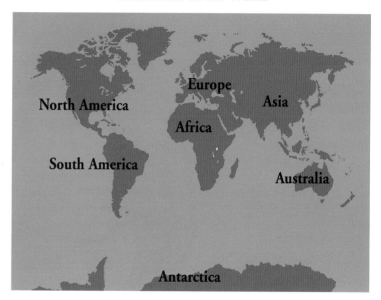

The world is divided into seven continents —
North America, South America, Europe, Africa,
Asia, Australia, and Antarctica. On the following
pages, the area where each animal lives is shown
in red, while all land is shown in green.

Words that appear in the glossary are printed in
boldface type the first time they occur in the text.

Harlequin Beetle

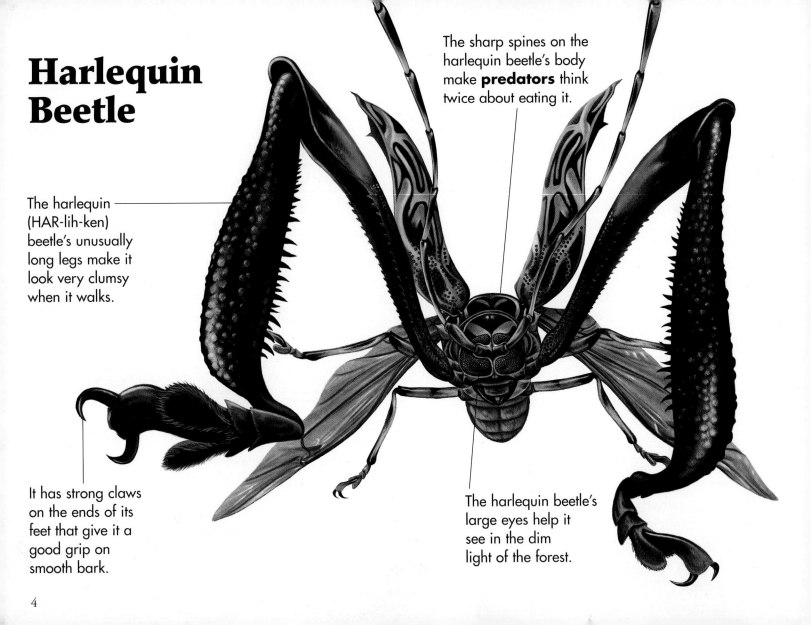

The sharp spines on the harlequin beetle's body make **predators** think twice about eating it.

The harlequin (HAR-lih-ken) beetle's unusually long legs make it look very clumsy when it walks.

It has strong claws on the ends of its feet that give it a good grip on smooth bark.

The harlequin beetle's large eyes help it see in the dim light of the forest.

Harlequin beetles begin life as eggs that **hatch** into **grubs**. The female harlequin beetle lays about fifteen eggs inside a hole in a tree trunk. These eggs hatch about ten days later. Thick, legless grubs emerge from the shells.

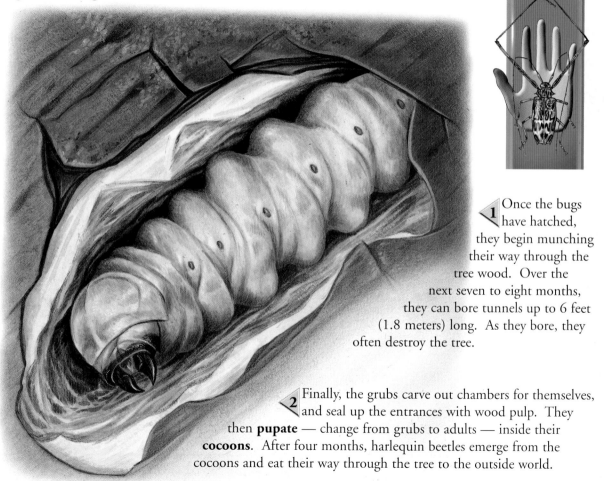

Size

1 Once the bugs have hatched, they begin munching their way through the tree wood. Over the next seven to eight months, they can bore tunnels up to 6 feet (1.8 meters) long. As they bore, they often destroy the tree.

2 Finally, the grubs carve out chambers for themselves, and seal up the entrances with wood pulp. They then **pupate** — change from grubs to adults — inside their **cocoons**. After four months, harlequin beetles emerge from the cocoons and eat their way through the tree to the outside world.

Did You Know?

The harlequin beetle is often covered with tiny **mites** that live off its body. The mites use a special glue to help them stick to the beetle when it flies.

Where in the World

Harlequin beetles live in the **tropical** forests of Central and South America and are also found in the Caribbean. In forests, adult harlequin beetles mainly eat tree **sap**.

Giant Millipede

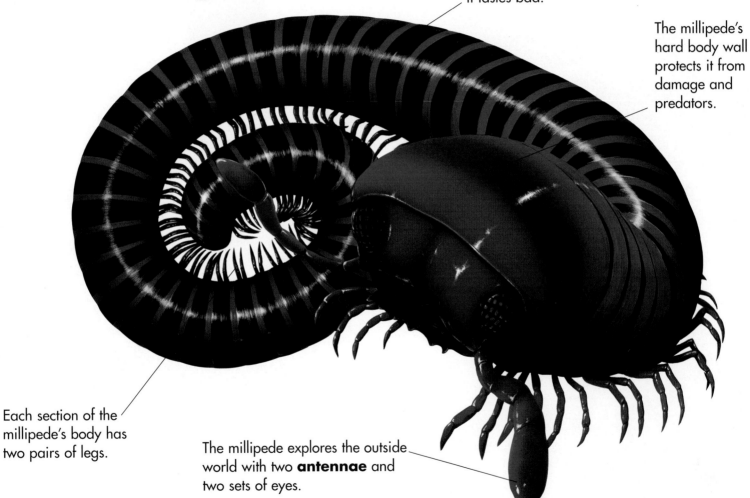

The millipede's (MIL-ih-peed) body is brightly colored to warn other animals that it tastes bad.

The millipede's hard body wall protects it from damage and predators.

Each section of the millipede's body has two pairs of legs.

The millipede explores the outside world with two **antennae** and two sets of eyes.

Millipedes have between two hundred and three hundred legs. Despite having so many legs, they move slowly. To defend themselves from predators, they ooze **toxin** from their colorful bodies.

1 A young, furry **tenrec** is hunting for a meal on the island of Madagascar off the eastern coast of Africa. It comes across a giant millipede and decides to eat it.

2 The millipede coils up so that only its hard outer body shell is exposed. Then it begins to squeeze toxin from special pores along its sides. The toxin gets into the tenrec's eyes, blinding it and making it run away in pain.

Size

Where in the World

Giant millipedes live in tropical parts of the world. Most are found in South America, central and southern Africa, and southern and Southeast Asia. They like hot and damp forests.

Hickory Horned Devil

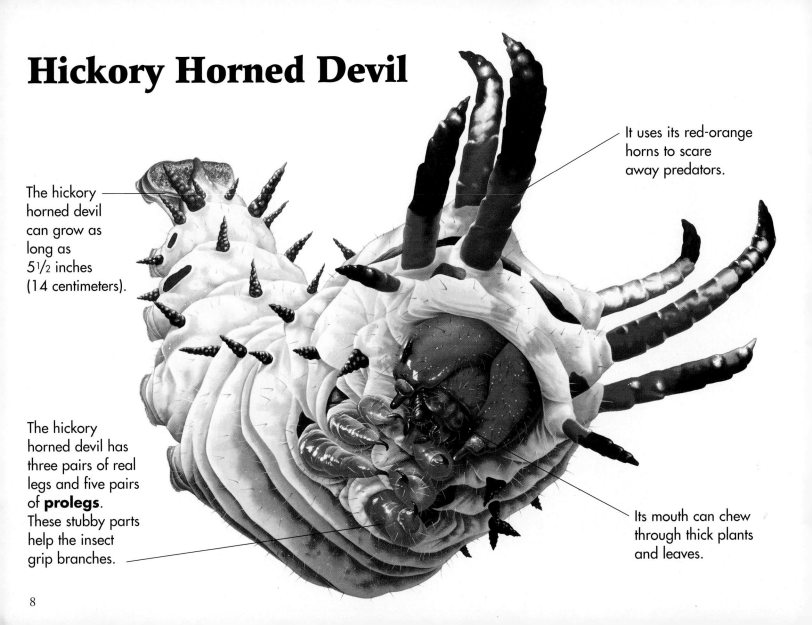

It uses its red-orange horns to scare away predators.

The hickory horned devil can grow as long as 5½ inches (14 centimeters).

The hickory horned devil has three pairs of real legs and five pairs of **prolegs**. These stubby parts help the insect grip branches.

Its mouth can chew through thick plants and leaves.

The hickory horned devil is not a dangerous animal and can be handled safely by humans. Its main defense against predators is its appearance, which can be very scary.

1 A chipmunk finds a hickory horned devil on a leaf. The chipmunk thinks that it might make a good meal, so it pokes it with its nose. The horned devil stays completely still, hoping that the chipmunk will leave it alone.

Size

2 The chipmunk does not give up. Suddenly, the horned devil rears up and shakes its head boldly from side to side. The sharp horns look very dangerous, so the chipmunk runs away to find an easier meal.

Where in the World

Hickory horned devils are found only in the eastern United States from New York State down to Florida and west to Kansas and Texas.

Hercules Beetle

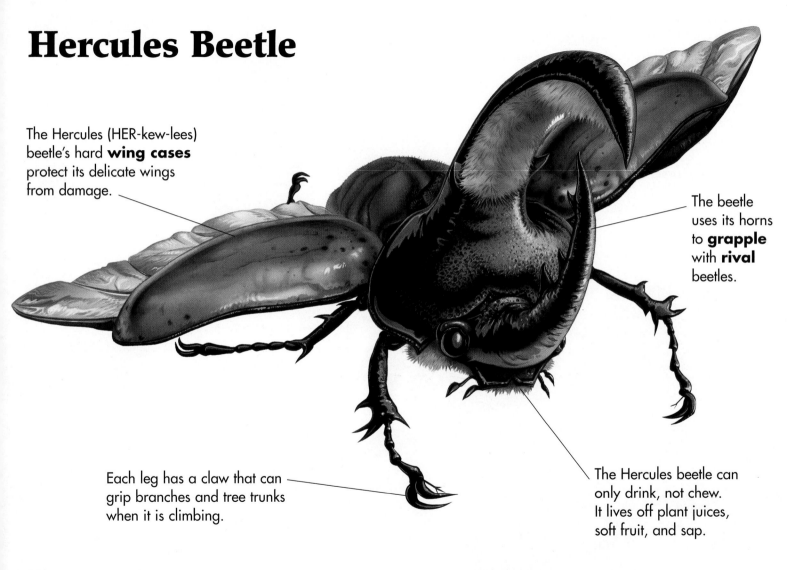

The Hercules (HER-kew-lees) beetle's hard **wing cases** protect its delicate wings from damage.

The beetle uses its horns to **grapple** with **rival** beetles.

Each leg has a claw that can grip branches and tree trunks when it is climbing.

The Hercules beetle can only drink, not chew. It lives off plant juices, soft fruit, and sap.

Hercules beetles have two horns shaped like the claws of a crab. These horns can grow up to 4 inches (10 cm) long. It uses them to fight other beetles.

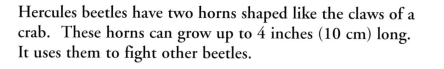

1 Two male Hercules beetles come head to head on a branch high above the **rain forest** floor. At first, each beetle tries to scare off the other by rubbing its wing cases against its **abdomen** to make a loud scraping sound.

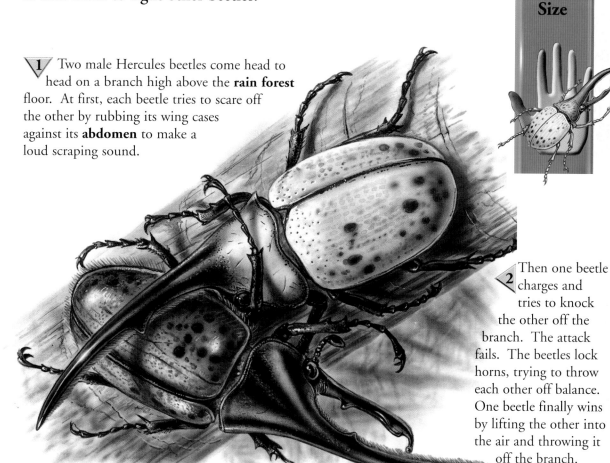

Size

2 Then one beetle charges and tries to knock the other off the branch. The attack fails. The beetles lock horns, trying to throw each other off balance. One beetle finally wins by lifting the other into the air and throwing it off the branch.

Where in the World

Hercules beetles live in Central and South America and also in the Caribbean Islands. Their **habitat** is the hot and damp tropical rain forest, where they can find plenty of plant food and water.

Goliath Beetle

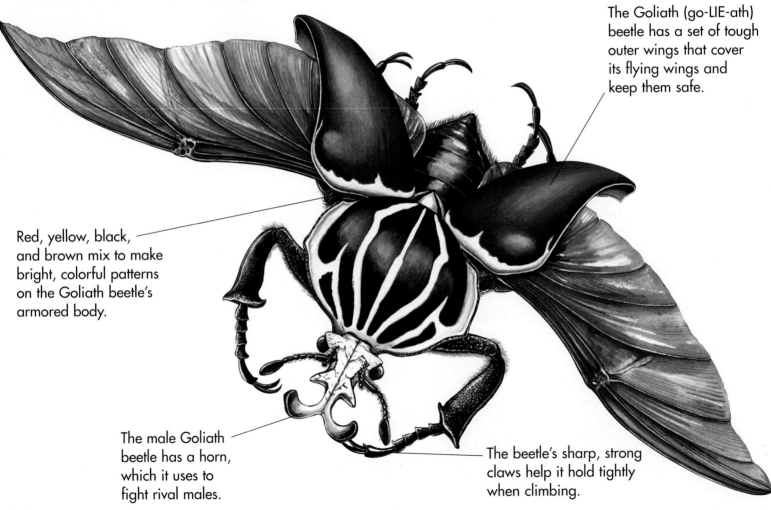

The Goliath (go-LIE-ath) beetle has a set of tough outer wings that cover its flying wings and keep them safe.

Red, yellow, black, and brown mix to make bright, colorful patterns on the Goliath beetle's armored body.

The male Goliath beetle has a horn, which it uses to fight rival males.

The beetle's sharp, strong claws help it hold tightly when climbing.

Goliath beetles grow a lot when they are grubs. During this stage of their lives, they are known as **larvae**. The grubs eat rotting plants.

Size

Goliath beetles can grip a branch so hard that it is even difficult for an adult human to pull them off. They grow to be 4 inches (10 cm) long.

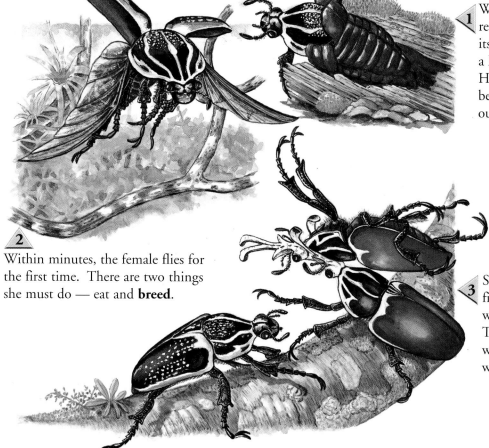

1 When the grub has reached its full size, its skin forms into a hard outer shell. Here, an adult female beetle finally breaks out of her shell.

2 Within minutes, the female flies for the first time. There are two things she must do — eat and **breed**.

3 She finds two males fighting each other with their horns. The beetle that wins will be able to **mate** with the female.

Where in the World

Goliath beetles live mainly in central and western Africa. They like to live in the tropical rain forests, where they can feed on plant sap.

13

Madagascar Hissing Cockroach

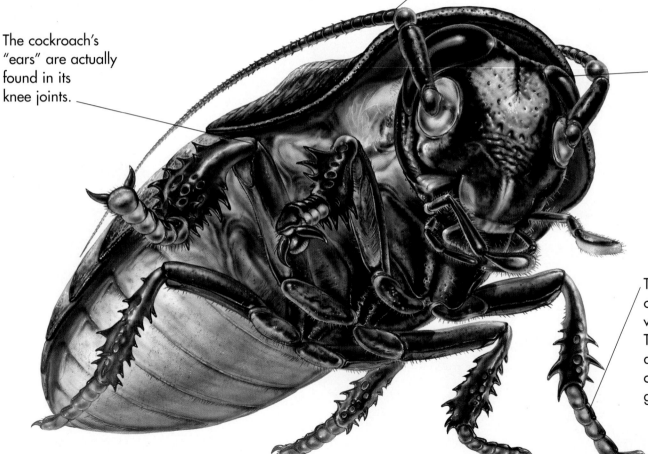

Each antenna of the Madagascar (mad-uh-GAS-kur) hissing cockroach is made up of up 130 parts. The antennae tells the cockroach about temperature, smells, and movement.

The cockroach's "ears" are actually found in its knee joints.

The hissing cockroach grows up to 3 inches (7.5 cm) long.

The hissing cockroach has very long legs. These help it move quickly and avoid obstacles on the ground.

Cockroaches make a tasty meal for many different types of predators, so they use speed and quick reactions to escape. The Madagascar hissing cockroach, however, also uses noise to scare away enemies.

Size

Did You Know?

The cockroach has a separate "brain" in its abdomen — which is why it can survive for several weeks even if its head has been cut off. Eventually, it dies from lack of food. Without a head, it cannot eat.

1 A **lemur** creeps along a branch in the rain forest. It is hunting a hissing cockroach farther along the branch. The lemur does not make any noise, but the cockroach has two **prongs** in its tail that detect movement. The prongs warn the cockroach of the approaching danger.

2 The lemur tries to grab the cockroach. To defend itself, the cockroach squeezes its abdomen tight, pushing air out through two openings on its sides. The air makes a very loud hiss that scares the lemur, which drops the cockroach and runs away.

Where in the World

There are more than one hundred species of cockroach, and they live all over the world. The Madagascar hissing cockroach lives on Madagscar, an island off the southeastern coast of Africa.

15

Huntsman Spider

The huntsman spider has very long legs, which it uses to chase prey.

The huntsman spider's head and body are very flat, which allows it to crawl into narrow gaps in rocks and logs.

The hairs on the spider's legs feel **vibrations** in the air, **alerting** it to predators.

Eight large eyes give the huntsman spider great eyesight, even in the dark.

Huntsman spiders can easily crawl up the steepest and most slippery surfaces — they can even climb up glass! Insects can find few hiding places that are safe from a huntsman.

1 A huntsman spider has spent the daytime hiding in a crack in a wall. Night falls, and the huntsman **emerges** to hunt for insects. It catches its **prey** by running fast, grabbing the insect, and stabbing it with its long fangs, which inject a **paralyzing venom**.

2 The huntsman's legs have strong claws. It uses these claws to cling to small cracks and ridges that people cannot see. The hairs on its legs trap water, which helps the spider "stick" to **vertical** surfaces.

Size

Where in the World

Huntsman spiders live in tropical islands in the Pacific Ocean. They are found in Australia, Tasmania, New Zealand, New Guinea, and Indonesia. They make homes under bark and rocks and also in the walls of buildings.

Stag Beetle

The male stag beetle needs a very large head to hold up its huge jaws.

The stag beetle uses its antennae to sense whatever is near it.

Its jaws have bumpy "teeth" that help it grip rival beetles.

Its legs end in strong claws. These are used for throwing and holding other beetles when fighting.

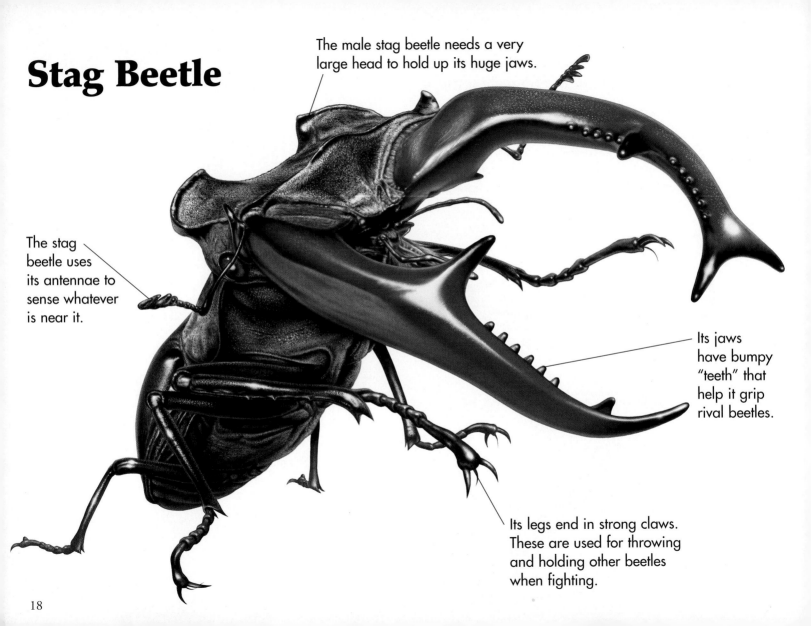

Male stag beetles often fight each other using their huge jaws. They usually fight over food and females. During their fights, each beetle will try to throw the other onto its back.

1 Two male stag beetles lock in **combat**. Their enormous jaws are not as powerful as they look. In fact, their jaw muscles are not strong enough to do much harm. Female stag beetles' jaws are much smaller, but their bite is much more painful.

Size

2 Each beetle uses its jaws to try to throw its rival onto its back. A beetle on its back can die if it cannot get onto to its feet. It either dries out in the sun or is killed by birds or other animals.

Did You Know?

Despite the stag beetle's ugly appearance, many people buy them to keep as pets. They can be very expensive animals. In 1999, a Japanese man paid $80,000 for just one giant stag beetle.

Where in the World

Stag beetles are found throughout much of southern and central Europe, from southern England in the west to Turkey in the east. Most other places in the world, however, have their own species of stag beetle.

Praying Mantis

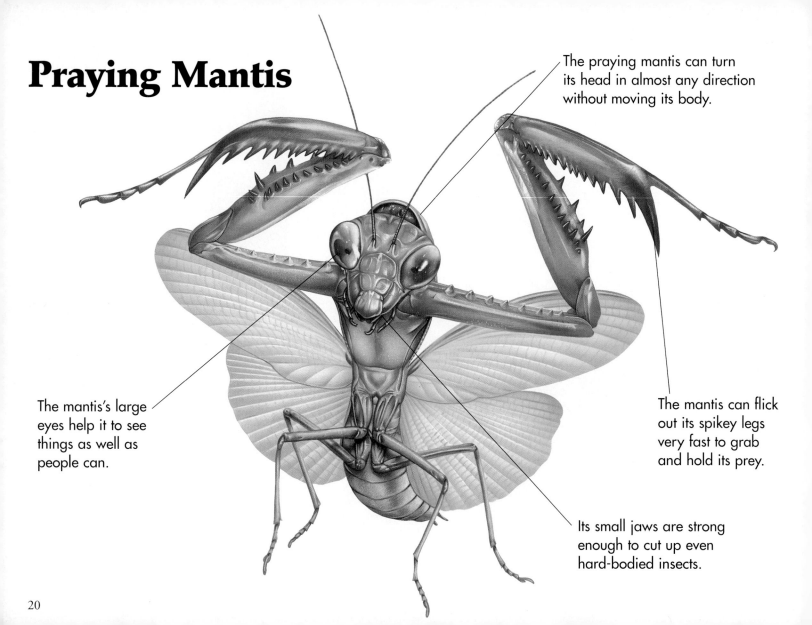

The praying mantis can turn its head in almost any direction without moving its body.

The mantis's large eyes help it to see things as well as people can.

The mantis can flick out its spikey legs very fast to grab and hold its prey.

Its small jaws are strong enough to cut up even hard-bodied insects.

Praying mantises eat other insects, especially butterflies and grasshoppers. In tropical parts of the world, however, they grow very large and eat frogs, lizards, and mice as well.

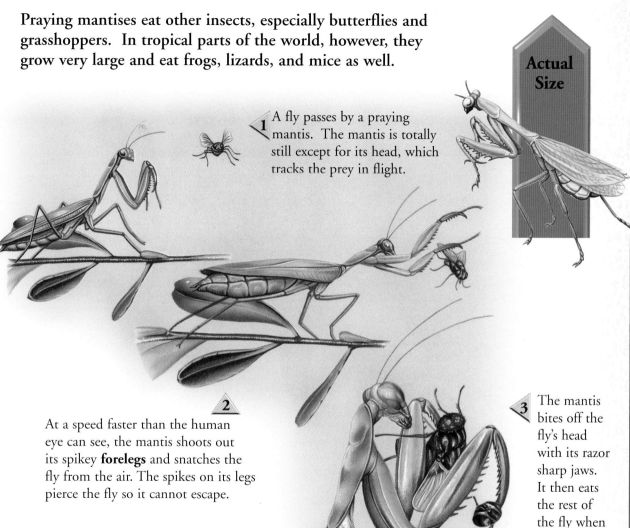

Actual Size

1 A fly passes by a praying mantis. The mantis is totally still except for its head, which tracks the prey in flight.

2 At a speed faster than the human eye can see, the mantis shoots out its spikey **forelegs** and snatches the fly from the air. The spikes on its legs pierce the fly so it cannot escape.

3 The mantis bites off the fly's head with its razor sharp jaws. It then eats the rest of the fly when it is hungry.

Where in the World

Praying mantises live in southern Europe, North Africa, and some parts of the United States. They are found among leaves, but their **camouflage** and their ability to stand completely still make them difficult to see.

21

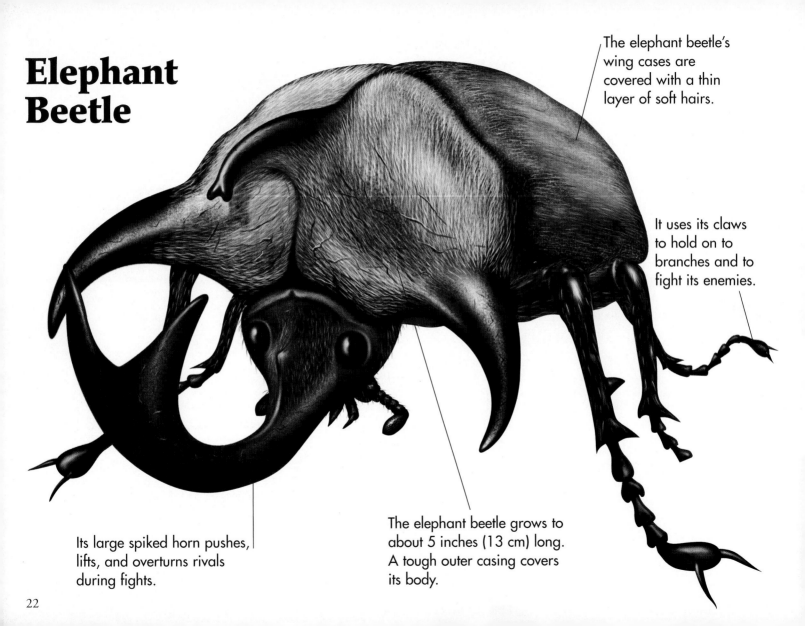

Elephant Beetle

The elephant beetle's wing cases are covered with a thin layer of soft hairs.

It uses its claws to hold on to branches and to fight its enemies.

Its large spiked horn pushes, lifts, and overturns rivals during fights.

The elephant beetle grows to about 5 inches (13 cm) long. A tough outer casing covers its body.

Male elephant beetles often fight each other. Sometimes, they fight over food, and at other times, they fight to mate with a female elephant beetle.

Size

△1 Two male elephant beetles moving along a branch meet each other head-on. They raise their horns and prepare to fight.

2 The beetles fight using their feet and horns. They grab hold with their clawed feet, attempting to throw each other off balance. They also try to get their horns underneath their rival's body to lift him into the air and flip him off the branch or onto his back. Eventually, one beetle throws the other to the ground.

Did You Know?

The elephant beetle has a relative called the rhinoceros beetle. In parts of Southeast Asia, beetle fights are a sport that large crowds of people watch. The people bet money on which one will win.

Where in the World

Elephant beetles live in Central America and northern South America. They like to live in the hot, damp rain forests, where the adults feed on sap from the trees and **nectar** from flowers.

23

Giant Orb Spider

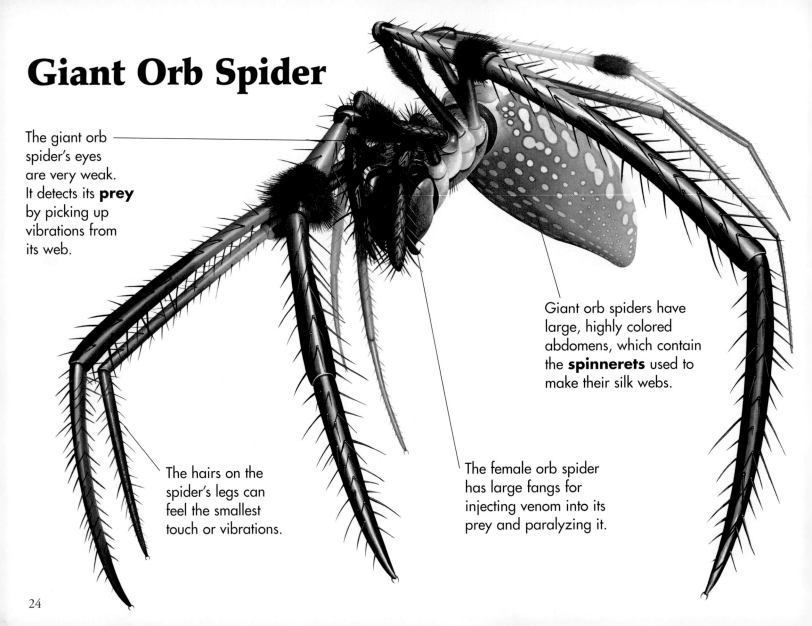

The giant orb spider's eyes are very weak. It detects its **prey** by picking up vibrations from its web.

Giant orb spiders have large, highly colored abdomens, which contain the **spinnerets** used to make their silk webs.

The hairs on the spider's legs can feel the smallest touch or vibrations.

The female orb spider has large fangs for injecting venom into its prey and paralyzing it.

Giant orb spiders weave huge webs. Some of the **strands** are 66 feet (20 m) long! The webs are so strong that native people in New Guinea use them as fishing nets.

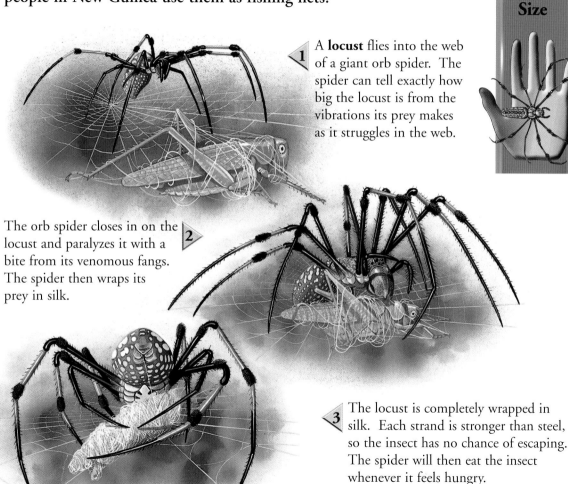

1 A **locust** flies into the web of a giant orb spider. The spider can tell exactly how big the locust is from the vibrations its prey makes as it struggles in the web.

2 The orb spider closes in on the locust and paralyzes it with a bite from its venomous fangs. The spider then wraps its prey in silk.

3 The locust is completely wrapped in silk. Each strand is stronger than steel, so the insect has no chance of escaping. The spider will then eat the insect whenever it feels hungry.

Size

Did You Know?

Female giant orb spiders are much, much bigger than males. A female can be as much as 2 inches (5 cm) long, but a male is less than one-fourth of an inch (6 millimeters) long.

Where in the World

Giant orb spiders live in many tropical parts of the world, including South and Central America, Africa, southern and Southeast Asia, and eastern Australia.

Giant Centipede

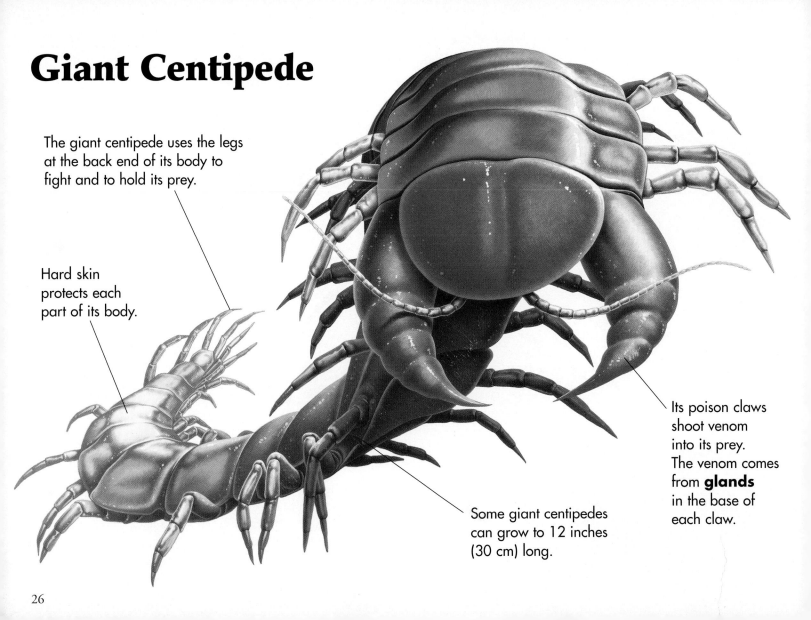

The giant centipede uses the legs at the back end of its body to fight and to hold its prey.

Hard skin protects each part of its body.

Its poison claws shoot venom into its prey. The venom comes from **glands** in the base of each claw.

Some giant centipedes can grow to 12 inches (30 cm) long.

The giant centipede's bite is very poisonous. If it bites a human, its venom causes terrible pain and **blistered** skin. Its venom is strong enough to kill birds, snakes, lizards, and mice.

1 A giant centipede creeps up on a small bird sitting on a branch. The centipede has found its prey using its antennae.

2 The centipede quickly attacks. It grabs the bird with its deadly claws.

3 The bird dies as the centipede pumps deadly venom into its body. Then the centipede curls around the bird and begins to eat it with its powerful cutting mouthparts.

Size

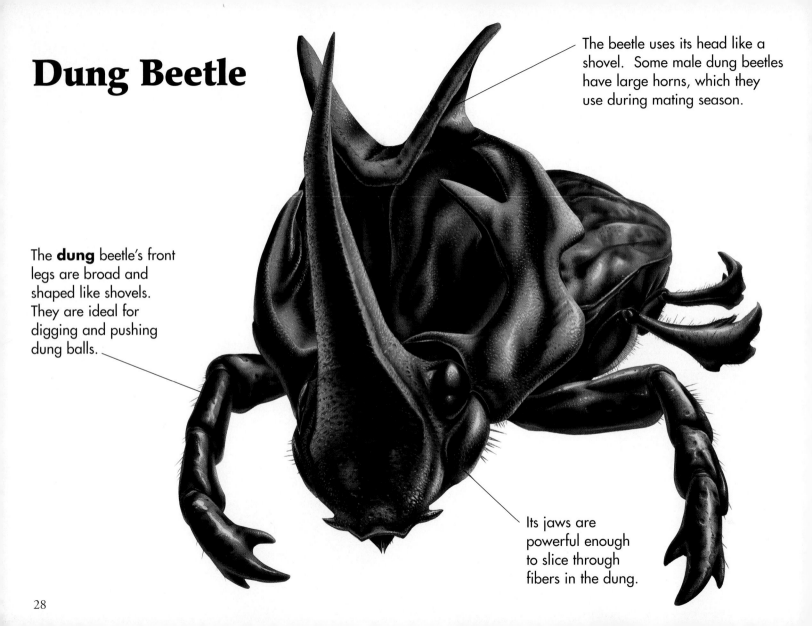

Dung Beetle

The beetle uses its head like a shovel. Some male dung beetles have large horns, which they use during mating season.

The **dung** beetle's front legs are broad and shaped like shovels. They are ideal for digging and pushing dung balls.

Its jaws are powerful enough to slice through fibers in the dung.

Dung beetles prefer to eat the dung of plant-eating animals, such as elephants, cattle, and antelopes. Beetles often try to steal each other's dung balls. Then the beetles fight.

Actual Size

1 The beetle shapes the dung into a big ball and starts to roll it away. Then another beetle flies down to steal the dung ball.

2 The owner of the dung ball hangs onto it with its back legs. It tries to fight off the newcomer. They fight, trying to flip each other over with their powerful front legs.

3 In this case, the newcomer wins and shoves the owner out of the way. It then begins to roll the ball off for itself.

Where in the World

The seven thousand different species of dung beetle live all over the world. They do not often live in cold or dry places because they need the droppings of plant-eating animals.

Glossary

abandoned — no longer in use, left behind
abdomen — the lower section of an insect's body
alerting — warning
antennae — a pair of long feelers on the head of insects or crustaceans, animals with a hard shell that live in water
blistered — covered with blisters, bubble-like bumps that swell up on the skin
breed — to join with the other sex to make babies
camouflage — the pattern on an animal's skin that helps to hide it
cocoons — sacs, pouches, or cases that help protect the larvae before they change into adults
combat — a fight
dung — the waste material of animals
emerges — comes out
forelegs — the front legs
glands — parts of the body that make special chemicals needed for the body to work properly
grapple — to wrestle with
grubs — another name for larvae
habitat — a place where an animal or plant lives
hatch — to break out of an egg
larvae — young, developing insects
lemur — an animal that lives in trees and is now mainly found in Madagascar
locust — a type of grasshopper that lives in a swarm
mate — to join together to make babies

mites — small spiderlike insects
mummies — bodies that have been carefully cleaned, dried, and wrapped in linen to preserve them after burial
nectar — a sweet liquid found in flowers
paralyzing — making it impossible for something to move
predators — animals that hunt, kill, and eat other animals
prey — an animal hunted for food
prolegs — fleshy legs that do not have joints
prongs — thin, pointed parts that stick out
pupa — an insect between larva and adult stages; during this time, the insect is often in a cocoon
pupate — turn into a pupa and change into an adult insect
rain forest — thick forest, often in tropical regions, where lots of rain falls
rival — competing
sap — the thick fluid that carries a plant's food
spinnerets — the parts of a spider's body that makes silk
strands — threads or fibers
tenrec — a small, spiny animal that eats insects
toxin — a poisonous substance
tropical — referring to the warmest regions of the world, with lush plant life and lots of rain
venom — poison
vertical — upright
vibrations — tiny motions caused by sounds or movements
wingcases — hard coverings that protect an insect's delicate flying wings

For More Information

Books

Beetles and Other Bugs. Amazing Bugs (series).
   Anna Clayborne (Stargazer Books)

Centipedes and Millipedes. Theresa Greenaway et al.
   (Steck-Vaugn)

*Everything Bug: What Kids Really Want to Know
   About Insects and Spiders.* Cherie Winner
   (Northwood Press)

Giant Book of Bugs and Creepy Crawlies.
   Jim Piper (Copper Beech)

*Simon & Schuster Children's Guide to Insects
   and Spiders.* Jinny Johnson (Simon & Schuster
   Children's Publishing)

Spiders, Centipedes and Millipedes. Sally Morgan
   (Chrysalis Education)

Spiders, Insects, and Minibeasts. Penny Clarke
   (Franklin Watts)

Web Sites

Arachnology.org
www.arachnology.org/Arachnology/Pages/Kids.html

Earthlife.net
www.earthlife.net/insects/six.html

Insect ID — Beetles
www.entomology.wisc.edu/insectid/beetle.php

Insects 4 Kids
homeschooling.gomilpitas.com/explore/bugs.htm

Insecta-inspecta.com
www.insecta-inspecta.com/beetles/scarab/index.html

Spider Identification Chart
www.termite.com/spider-identification.html

The World of Giant Insects
www.kokorodinosaurs.com/giantinsects.html

Publisher's note to educators and parents: Our editors have
carefully reviewed these Web sites to ensure that they are suitable for
children. Many Web sites change frequently, however, and we cannot
guarantee that a site's future contents will continue to meet our high
standards of quality and educational value. Be advised that children
should be closely supervised whenever they access the Internet.

Index